NATIONAL GEOGRAPHIC

Ladders

Common Core

Worth saving

EVERY LIVING THING

by Shirleyann Costigan

Living things are cool. The bark spider can spin a web across a river. Its silk is super strong! The rosy periwinkle is used to make drugs that treat illnesses. The gribble is a tiny worm with a big secret. It may help to make a clean fuel.

Bark spider

Rosy periwinkle

Gribble

Luckily, these helpful **species** are not threatened with **extinction.** Extinction is the complete loss of a species, which happens when the last living member of a species dies. Extinction is nothing new. Almost all species that have ever lived have become extinct. Many species are **endangered,** or at risk of becoming extinct.

Extinct species are not cool. If a species becomes extinct, we will never know how it may have helped us.

But what if an endangered species cannot help humans. Is it not worth saving?

How Endangered Is It?

EXTINCT
last member of the species has died

EXTINCT IN THE WILD
survives only in captivity

CRITICALLY ENDANGERED
extremely high risk of extinction

ENDANGERED
very high risk of extinction

VULNERABLE
high risk of extinction

NEAR THREATENED
moving toward high risk of extinction

LEAST CONCERN
no immediate threat to survival

The terms on the left are from the "Red List of Threatened Species." The list comes from the International Union for the **Conservation** of Nature. It helps conservationists plan ways to save species that are at risk.

Why are so many species at risk? The biggest threat to species is **habitat** loss. Most habitat loss is caused by humans. People may destroy species' habitats when they clear land for buildings or farming. Pollution and climate change can also destroy a species' habitat. The next pages show threats that endanger many species.

Aye-Aye Lemur

The aye-aye is a primate. Apes are also primates. The aye-aye lives in Madagascar, but growing cities threaten its habitat. Some people kill the aye-aye because they think it is bad luck.

Asian Tapir

The Asian tapir looks like a pig with a trunk. It is losing its habitat in the rain forests of Southeast Asia. More than half of the Asian tapirs have died since 1970.

ENDANGERED

Parts of Southeast Asia

NEAR THREATENED

Parts of Madagascar

Star Cactus

People take this pretty cactus from the wild and sell it as a houseplant. That's one reason it is at risk. Conservationists are working to save the star cactus. They are growing it to sell, so people will stop taking it from the wild.

VULNERABLE

Border of Mexico and the U.S.

Wyoming Toad

People thought the Wyoming Toad was extinct. Then a group was found and used to start a breeding program. The program produces new toads. Today, new toads are still released into the wild, but they face many challenges.

EXTINCT IN THE WILD

Wyoming, U.S.

Green Pitcher Plant

The leaves of this plant are like tubes. Insects fall into the tubes. Then the plant digests the insects. It gets nutrients from the insects, so it can live in soil that has few nutrients. But can it live with threats from farming, housing, and recreation?

CRITICALLY ENDANGERED

Southeastern U.S.

Sapphire-bellied Hummingbird

This tiny bird lives in the tropical forests of Colombia. Toxic chemicals and habitat loss threaten the hummingbird. Hawks and other large birds threaten it, too.

CRITICALLY ENDANGERED

The coast of Colombia

Giant Weta

Wetas have lived on Earth since before the dinosaurs. Now, this species is in danger. Habitat loss and predators may cause its extinction.

Harlequin Mantella Frog

Hunters for the pet trade capture hundreds of these frogs each year. Logging and other industries have destroyed most of its habitat. Today, only a few of this colorful species still exist.

Columbia Pygmy Rabbit

This rabbit was so tiny, it could fit in your hand. A dam on the Columbia River changed this species' habitat. The rabbit couldn't adapt to the change. The last of the species died in 2010.

EXTINCT

Washington, U.S.

Saola

Some people call this ox the Asian unicorn. Hunters were killing it for its meat in the early 1990s. Since then, people have made plans to protect the endangered species. Hunters are still a threat, though. Today, fewer than 300 saolas exist.

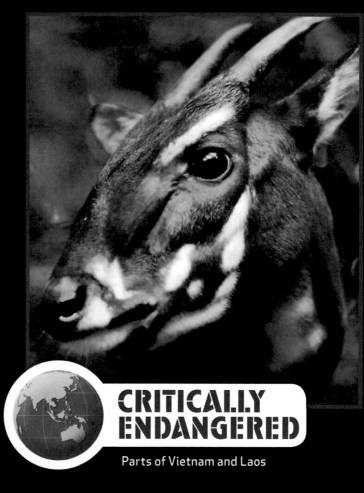

CRITICALLY ENDANGERED

Parts of Vietnam and Laos

Oregon Chub Minnow

The Oregon Fish and Wildlife Service rescued this little fish from extinction. The minnows were moved from threatened habitats to safer waters. Today the little fish are thriving!

VULNERABLE

Oregon, U.S.

Mekong Giant Catfish

This ten-foot, 400-pound fish swims in a river in China and is a favorite food there. Overfishing and habitat loss caused by the building of dams are two reasons that it's critically endangered.

CRITICALLY ENDANGERED

Vietnam and Laos

Joel Sartore

Today many groups work to save endangered species. Individuals are helping too. One of these individuals is a photographer named Joel Sartore.

Joel Sartore photographs endangered animals for the National Geographic Society. He has traveled around the world to photograph different species. His photographs remind us that every single creature matters.

Baby caiman

Check In What do you think makes a species worth saving?

Saving Puldunny Pond

by Evelyn Stone   illustrated by Nicholas Jackson

If I could speak fish, I would say, "Thank you, Oregon chub minnow, for making me a hero."

My name is Kenny and I live in Puldunny, Oregon. Puldunny is a small town, but it has a school, a town hall, a main street, and a pond.

Every summer, the Youth Center sponsors a project for kids who are looking for something to do. This year's theme was "Let's **Preserve** Puldunny," and eleven kids volunteered.

The day before the project started, I went to the pond with my friend Felicia. I call her Flea, but she doesn't mind. Flea and I wanted to collect bugs, but the mosquitoes saw us coming. We got bitten up! We collected a few bugs and got outta' there.

The next day we were covered in welts. "Mosquito bites,"
Flea explained to the project team, "from the pond."

"Mosquitoes can carry disease," Jamie Ealing said. "I
never go near that pond."

"Soon you might not be able to," said Amy Franc. "My dad
said the town council is talking about draining it."

"Yes-s-s-s!" Budgie Ricks yelled. "I hope they put in a
skateboard park!"

"Okay, kids," said Ms. Garcia. "Let's plan our project. It
must preserve some part of the community, and it can't cost
money. Any ideas?"

Jamie raised his hand. "What about Puldunny Pond?" If we got rid of the mosquitoes, maybe we could save it."

"Fat chance," said Budgie.

"Shhh!" said Flea. "It's a good idea."

Ms. Garcia agreed. "Puldunny Pond is a rich **habitat,** but it would be impossible to get rid of the mosquitoes."

So I said, "What about the Oregon chub?"

Then all eyes were on me.

The Oregon Chub Minnow

Scale
Mouth
Fin
Gill

Pacific Ocean

Willamette Basin

Habitats: small ponds, marshes, slou...
Distribution: Willamette Valley
Spawning season spans from
April through September
Predators: bullfrog,
largemouth bass, others
Diet: Chironomid larvae
(midge, mosquito),
Copepods, Rotifers

Diet

Chironomid larvae
(midge, mosquito)

Copepods

"Yes, Kenny, go on," said Ms. Garcia.

"The Oregon chub minnow is a **species** of fish. It was **endangered** until the Fish and Wildlife Service moved it to new habitats." We could get some minnows for Puldunny Pond. The minnows would eat the mosquitoes. Moving the minnows is free."

"Maybe we could get some minnows for Puldunny Pond. They would eat the mosquitoes, and moving them is free."

"That's a great idea," said Flea. "Because . . ."

"Because Kenny's your boyfriend," Budgie sang.

"Because," Flea went on, "maybe we could save the pond and help keep the minnow off the endangered species list."

"Yes," said Ms. Garcia. "Kenny, contact the Fish and Wildlife Service and find out the **requirements** for the Oregon chub minnow's habitat."

So I found out what the fish needs in its habitat. The water has to be just the right temperature and less than six feet deep. It can't have any chemicals or non-native fish because they might eat the minnows, and . . . the list went on and on.

"We can't do it," I told the team. "There are too many requirements. Puldunny Pond is not the right habitat."

"It might be," said Flea. "Let's go to the pond and find out for sure."

"It won't work," said Budgie.

"Maybe it won't," Ms. Garcia said, "but we should try."

The next day, covered in special clothing and bug spray, we marched to the pond. Amy Franc's dad came, too, and he brought his rowboat.

We measured the depth and temperature of the pond and collected samples. We made a list of the plants, fish, and insects we saw. Back at the Youth Center, we wrote a report that had lists, graphs, and the names of the species we found. It took days! Sometimes, Budgie snuck out, but Ms. Garcia said he'd be an endangered species if he did it again. Finally we finished our report and sent to the Fish and Wildlife Service.

A week later, two men from the Fish and Wildlife Service took more samples from the pond. Then they asked us a few questions. Did they think it would work?

Finally, Ms. Garcia heard back from the Oregon Fish and Wildlife Service. Five hundred Oregon chubs would be moved to Puldunny Pond!

Amy Franc's dad had more good news. "The town council decided not to vote on draining the pond," he said. "We are going to wait until next summer." He saw me scratch a mosquito bite and said, "We'll send you to the pond, Kenny. If you come back without any bites, then we'll know that your plan worked!"

We all watched as the fish were released into the pond. Flea said I was a hero because the minnow idea was mine. She even gave me a new name. She calls me Chub.

Now if only I could speak fish.

Check In How did Kenny and the other children solve their problem?

STARS
Wild and Free

by Grace O'Brien
illustrated by Matt Luxich

A group of animals met in the wilderness. Most had never gone outside their own **habitats,** but an urgent mission brought them all together.

"Our **species** are at risk," said HB, the helmeted hornbill. "Humans call us **'endangered'** or 'threatened,' but they aren't helping us! They help furry and beautiful **'celebrity'** animals, like pandas and penguins. We're going to change that!"

The animals cheered. They were not celebrities, and they were not furry or beautiful. Some had spines, some had odd features, and some seemed too tiny to matter.

HB went on, "We may not be celebrities, but we are STARS—Super Terrific At-Risk Species." Then he asked the animals, "Who are we?"

"STARS!" they shouted.

HB introduced the speakers. The animals listened as a duck-billed platypus, an aye-aye lemur, and a tapir told about threats to their species. As the STARS spoke, a video screen showed the locations of their habitats.

"And now, one final speaker!" said HB. A Mekong giant catfish appeared on the screen. He was almost one hundred years old, but a school of fish had taught him how to video chat.

Bubble, bubble. "Don't give up!" he said. "Humans can help. Tell them your stories, and spread your stories around the world."

STARS
SUPER TERRIFIC AT-RISK SPECI

The catfish's speech gave the
animals hope. They had to think
of a plan to help them all avoid
extinction . . . *fast!*

"He's right," said Edna, the echidna. "We need to tell our stories to humans. What if we use a camera, like Mr. Mekong did?" Edna knew her plan would work.

So the STARS got to work. They began filming a documentary to tell their stories. They filmed all over the world. They wanted to show how their habitats and lives were in danger.

A year later, the documentary was ready, but more STARS and habitats were at risk.

Back in the wild, HB wondered, "How can we get humans to watch our documentary?" Just then, a pair of binoculars fell from above.

HB looked up and saw a human in a tree. The human was looking for the at-risk species.

"Oh my!" she cried, and then she climbed down.

HB gasped, but then he remembered what the catfish said. *Humans can help. Tell them your stories.* So HB took a deep breath and told the human about how his habitat had changed and about the STARS' mission. The other animals told their stories, too.

The woman said, "I'm a scientist. I help endangered species, and I'd like to help you."

The animals were excited. They kept talking with the scientist and planned to show the documentary to humans in a city far away.

The animals arrived in the city a few weeks later. What a strange, new habitat! They felt nervous, but they trusted the scientist, so they followed her into a building that said "National Geographic Society."

Inside, they met the scientist's friends, who were ready to see a documentary about at-risk species. The human in charge led them all into a room with a big screen and lots of posters of documentaries showing celebrity animals on the walls.

"These humans have made a lot of movies," he thought, "but I don't see any with STARS! If they could show our documentary, our species might have a chance."

Edna started the film and the lights went out. When the lights came back on, the human in charge turned to HB and said, "This film is amazing! I love it! What should we call it?"

"How about *STARS Wild and Free?*" said HB.

"You've got it!" cried the human.

Soon, movie posters showing STARS were hanging everywhere. The movie was a big hit, and humans started finding ways to save these amazing animals.

Check In How did the STARS solve their problem?

Discuss — Cause and Effect and Point of View

1. According to "Every Living Thing," what is the main cause of habitat loss?

2. Choose one species in "Every Living Thing." What is the effect of habitat loss on this species?

3. Identify the point of view from which "Saving Puldunny Pond" and "STARS Wild and Free" are told. Which is first-person? Which is third-person? Compare and contrast the point of view.

4. If you had to choose one species to protect, which species would it be? Why?